THE GREAT ANIMAL SEARCH

Caroline Young

Illustrated by
Ian Jackson

Designed by
Andy Dixon

Series editor:
Felicity Brooks

Scientific consultants:
Dr Margaret Rostron
Dr John Rostron

Blue whales are the biggest animals of all. You'll find one on pages 34 and 35.

Gardens are busy places. Pages 36 and 37 show you what might live there.

Pigs are just one of the animals you can see on pages 38 and 39.

Find out how a shingle-backed skink gets rid of enemies on pages 32 and 33.

Bright flame shrimps live on the Barrier Reef, on pages 30 and 31.

Tigers hunt in the thick jungles of India. Find out what else lives there on pages 28 and 29.

Snow leopards hunt in the highest places. Turn to pages 26 and 27 to find out where.

Starfish live on the seashore. Find out what else does on pages 24 and 25.

Contents

Squirrels are just one of the animals living in woods like the one on pages 22 and 23.

The huge African plains on pages 20 and 21 are home to fast-running cheetahs.

About this book

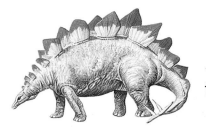

This creature is a Stegosaurus. Turn to pages 4 and 5 to find out about more kinds of dinosaurs.

You can find out about more than 300 different kinds of animals in this book, but it's not just a book about animals. It's a puzzle book, too. This is how the puzzles work, plus a few tips to help you solve them.

Skunks make their home in the thick conifer forests on pages 6 and 7.

There are around 100 animals in each big picture. In real life, there would not be as many in the same place at the same time.

Around the outside of each big picture, there are lots of little pictures.

The writing next to each one tells you how many of that animal you can find in the big picture.

American bald eagles glide above the swamps on pages 8 and 9.

North Africa
African plains

Female elephants and babies live together. Male elephants live along. Find seven.

Many of the world's best-known animals live in Africa, on huge, grassy plains. There are 17 kinds of animals here.

If you look closely, you can see what each kind eats. Most eat grass and leaves. Some kill other animals to eat.

Ostriches are birds, but they can't fly. Find three ostriches and their nest.

Hippos enjoy soaking in mud. It stops their skin from drying out. Find six.

Giraffes can reach food that no other animal can get to. Find four giraffes.

If a zebra sees an enemy, it barks, to warn the others. Spot eight zebras.

Cheetahs run faster than any other animal, but they can't do it for long. Spot two.

Gerenuks can stand up on their back legs to reach the tastiest food. Spot two.

When vultures are flying, they can spot a meal a long way away. Spot nine vultures.

Warthogs snuffle along, digging up food with their long tusks. Spot three.

Wild dogs roam the plains, searching for something to eat. Spot eight.

Thomson's gazelles jump and flash their white bottoms to confuse enemies. Spot ten.

Big groups of wildebeest wander across the plains, looking for food. Find eight.

If enemies attack rhinos, they charge at them, horn first. Spot three rhinos.

Baboon babies often ride on their parents' backs. Find eight baboons.

Male lions look fierce, but lionesses do the most hunting. Spot six lions.

Kori bustards are the heaviest flying birds on Earth. Can you find two bustards here?

Leopards often drag their food up into a tree to eat it in peace. Find two leopards.

20 / 21

This giraffe's horn counts as one giraffe.

A lioness has killed this zebra, but the zebra still counts.

This baby baboon counts as one baboon.

These elephants in the distance count.

Tarantulas like heat. They live in the Sonoran Desert on pages 10 and 11.

The puzzly part is finding all the animals. Some are easy to spot, but some are tiny, or hidden against their background. On some pages there's another puzzle too.

If you get stuck, you'll find all the answers on pages 40-45. Every single animal shown in the little pictures that you can find in each big picture counts in your total.

Polar bears live in the Arctic. Find out what else lives there on pages 12 and 13.

Camels live in the scorching Sahara Desert. Spot more of them on pages 18 and 19.

Sloths find it easy to hide in the thick Amazon Rainforest on pages 16 and 17.

Octopuses are just one of the sea creatures you can find out about on pages 14 and 15.

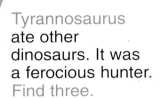

Tyrannosaurus ate other dinosaurs. It was a ferocious hunter. Find three.

Back in time

Alamosaurus lived on marshy land, munching plants. Find two.

Seventy million years ago, part of North America probably looked like this. Animals called dinosaurs lived here. There are 51 creatures for you to find in this picture. Can you spot them all?

Pteranodon flew on big wings of stretched-out skin. Find two others here.

Parasaurolophus had a curved, bony tube on its head. Can you spot three?

Struthiomimus looked a bit like an ostrich without feathers. Spot seven.

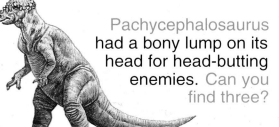

Pachycephalosaurus had a bony lump on its head for head-butting enemies. Can you find three?

Maiasauras laid their eggs in nests. Find one Maiasaura.

4

Deinosuchus' name means "terrible crocodile". Spot two.

Styracosaurus had a bony collar around its neck. Find one.

Ankylosaurus swung its bony tail like a club. Find two.

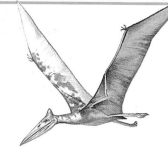
Quetzalcoatlus was a pterosaur, or "flying lizard". It was as big as a small plane. Spot two.

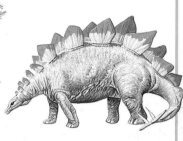
Stegosaurus had bony plates along its back to protect it from enemies. Find two.

Panoplosaurus was covered with knobs and spikes. Find five.

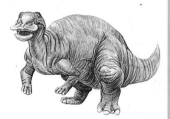
Anatosaurus had a kind of beak instead of a mouth. Spot three.

Corythosaurus had a hollow, bony plate on its head. Spot four.

Triceratops looked fierce, but it spent its time eating. Find two.

Dromaeosaurus stabbed its enemies with its sharp claws. Spot six.

Conifer forests

Skunks spray smelly liquid at their enemies. Find three.

Black bears are good at climbing trees. Even the cubs can do it. Find four bears.

Snowshoe hares have furry feet to run in the deep snow in winter. Spot six hares.

Lynxes' beautiful coats blend with the shadows. Can you find three lynxes?

Spruce grouse only eat leaves and buds from spruce trees. Can you find four grouse?

Wolverines are also known as "gluttons". This means greedy people. Find three.

Forests cover the top of North America and Canada. The trees in them are mainly conifer trees that keep their leaves all year. Not many people live there, but lots of animals do. Can you spot 80 animals in this picture?

North American martens are fast and fierce hunters. Find three martens.

Chipmunks eat all summer, and sleep all winter. Find eight.

Northern shrikes spend all day feeding their babies. Find two.

Long-eared owls have two feathery tufts on their heads. Find four.

Beavers **can cut down trees with their sharp teeth.** Spot eight beavers.

Crossbills **have hooked beaks to dig seeds out of fir cones.** Find two.

Moose **can wade through water with their long, thin legs.** Find six moose.

Fishers **attack porcupines. They bite their soft tummies.** Spot four fishers.

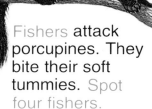
Brown bears **teach their cubs what to eat.** Find two and a cub.

Flying squirrels **can glide between trees.** Spot five squirrels.

Mink **slink along, looking for voles and insects to eat. Can you find three mink?**

Pumas **are also called mountain lions or cougars.** Spot three.

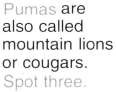

Ospreys **swoop into water to catch fish.** Find three.

Porcupines **are covered in spikes called quills.** Spot three.

Steamy swamps

Green tree frogs have suckers on their feet to climb slimy branches. Find eight frogs.

Otters can even eat fish while swimming on their backs. Spot six.

Snail kites only like eating one kind of snail. Can you find two snail kites?

Zebra butterfly. Spot four.

Fisher spiders eat insects clinging to the bottom of plant stems. Spot one.

Alligators Spot six.

Swamps are so wet you can't tell what is land and what is water. Many animals live in these watery worlds.

This picture shows part of a swamp in Florida, in the US, called the Everglades. Can you find 85 animals here?

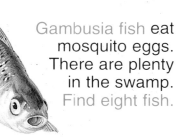

Gallinules are shy. They hide from enemies in the grass. Find four gallinules.

Gambusia fish eat mosquito eggs. There are plenty in the swamp. Find eight fish.

Bullfrog. Find three.

Bald eagles scoop fish up with their sharp claws. Find two.

Terrapins stick their skinny necks above water to take a look. Find ten.

Little blue herons wait for ages before spearing a fish. Spot two.

Raccoons use their front paws to scoop up fish and frogs from the water. Find six.

Cottonmouth snakes wiggle their bodies to swim along. Spot five.

Orb web spiders spin webs to catch passing insects. Find one.

Snapping turtles are experts at snapping up fish. Can you spot four turtles?

Anhingas dive underwater and stab fish with their beaks. Spot three.

Manatees swim slowly along, munching plants. Spot four.

Pileated woodpeckers keep their babies hidden. Spot three.

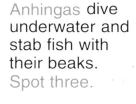

Garpike can easily tear up food with their sharp teeth. Spot three.

9

Dusty deserts

Trapdoor spiders crouch in tunnels and grab insects. Spot two.

Coyotes often howl to each other to keep in touch. Can you find six?

Desert tortoises hide under the sand all day to stay cool. Spot four.

Burrowing owls move into empty burrows rather than dig them. Spot six.

Mexican red-kneed bird eating spiders are poisonous, but only enough to kill an insect. Find six.

Life is hard in the scorching deserts of North America. One part of them is so hot that it's called Death Valley.

This picture shows part of the Sonoran Desert. If you look closely, you'll spot 95 animals that live in this dusty place.

Loggerhead shrikes push lizards onto cactus spikes. Spot four shrikes.

Black-tailed jackrabbits hop across the hot sand. Spot six jackrabbits.

Gila monsters lick insects' footprints to find them. Find four.

Gambel's quails blend in well with the desert. Can you find two?

Kangaroo rats get all the water they need from grains. Find six kangaroo rats.

Crafty gila woodpeckers build nests inside cacti. Spot seven.

Rattlesnakes shake their tails to make a scary rattle. Find three rattlesnakes.

Elf owls often move into empty woodpeckers' nests. Find five.

American fringe-toed lizards dig in the sand with their noses and toes. Find eight.

Swallow-tailed butterfly. Find six.

Roadrunners run in zig-zags, to confuse enemies. Spot three more.

Kit foxes, or swift foxes, run very swiftly across the sand. Find three foxes.

Chuckwallas hide between rocks. Enemies can't see them. Can you spot three?

Peccaries can even eat cacti with their tough teeth. Find ten peccaries.

The Arctic

Thick fur keeps polar bears warm. Spot three and two cubs.

Musk oxen don't mind snow. Their thick coats keep them warm. Can you spot nine?

In the Arctic, winter is so cold that the sea freezes. Many animals go to warmer places until spring. This picture shows the Arctic at the end of a long, cold winter. There are 101 animals here for you to spot.

Humpback whales like this one visit the Arctic. They "sing" as they swim.

Lemmings live in cosy tunnels under the snow all winter. Find 11.

Stoats even squeeze into lemmings' tunnels. Find three stoats.

Baby seals have pale fur which drops out after a few weeks. Spot four.

Ptarmigans are white in winter and brown in summer. Can you find five?

Arctic ground squirrel. Find three.

Snowy owls hunt during the long Arctic day. Find three.

Raven. Find three.

Narwhals have a horn sticking out above their mouths. Spot two narwhals.

Arctic foxes bury animals in the snow. It's like a freezer. Find five.

Wolves often hunt in a team called a pack. Spot ten.

Killer whales only kill fish and seals for food. Find two.

Walruses have plenty of fat to keep them warm. Find 12.

Caribou dig up plants under the snow. Spot 11 caribou.

Five kinds of seals live in the Arctic. Find one of each kind.

Harp seal

Ribbon seal

Ringed seal

Hooded seal

Bearded seal

White fur disguises Arctic hares very well. Find four others.

Beluga whale babies turn white when they are two. Find a mother and baby.

Under the sea

Fin whales swim along with their mouths open, swallowing food. Spot one.

Jellyfish sting small fish with their tentacles, then eat them. Find four jellyfish.

Angler fish wave a small fin above their mouths. Fish bite it and then get eaten. Find three.

These fishes' bodies light up in the gloomy deep water. Spot five of each kind.

Hatchet fish

Lantern fish

Gulper eels can gulp down fish which are bigger than themselves. Find two eels.

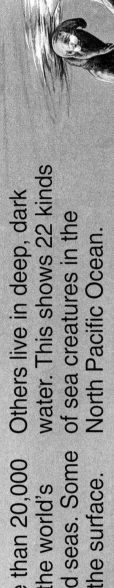

There are more than 20,000 kinds of fish in the world's rivers, lakes and seas. Some fish swim near the surface.

Others live in deep, dark water. This shows 22 kinds of sea creatures in the North Pacific Ocean.

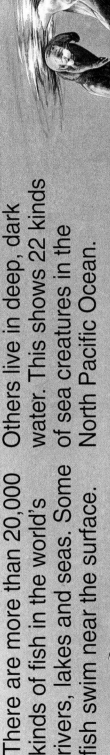

If an octopus is being chased, it squirts out cloudy brown ink. Can you spot two?

Sponge

Sea lily

Sea spider

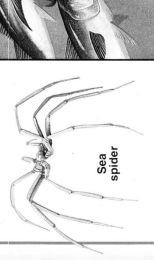

It is cold and dark at the bottom of the sea. Spot three of each of these creatures there.

Fishermen catch marlin. Their sharp noses can be dangerous. Spot two.

Squid have ten arms with suckers on them to catch fish. Spot ten squid.

Huge basking sharks float near the surface of the sea. Can you spot one?

Dolphins often leap above the water. Nobody knows why. Spot four dolphins.

If skates are disturbed, they give enemies electric shocks. Find three.

Sea otters break open shells to eat the creatures inside. Find five otters.

Herring

Tuna

Sand eel

Giant squid have big eyes to help them see in deep water. Find two.

Dall's porpoises swim fast. You can see their spray from far away. Find five.

Beard-worms. Can you spot a group?

Groups of these fish swim near the surface. Spot a group of each.

Tapirs use their long noses to sniff for food among the bushes. Find three.

Emerald tree boas slither through the green trees. They are hard to spot. Find three.

Uakari monkey Spot six.

Sloths move very slowly. They can spend their whole lives in one tree. Spot three.

Humming-birds move their wings quickly and make a humming sound. Find three.

Rainforests

Hoatzins are strange birds. They smell awful. Spot two and a baby.

In rainforests, it rains almost every day. Trees and plants grow incredibly fast. This shows part of the Amazon Rainforest in Brazil. More kinds of animals and plants live here than anywhere else. Can you find 71 animals?

Toucans live in pairs. Their huge beaks are made of hollow bone. Spot four.

Black howler monkeys howl to each other to keep in touch. Spot four.

Silky anteaters look for ants. They lick them up with their long tongues. Find two.

Capybaras are good swimmers. They spend most of their time in the water. Spot ten.

Golden lion tamarins have manes of golden hair, like lions. Find three.

Golden cock-of-the-rock. Spot two.

Jaguars climb trees and swim across rivers to catch animals. Find one.

Anacondas can squeeze animals to death. Then they eat them whole. Find three.

Giant armadillos have thick, scaly skin to keep teeth and claws out. Spot two.

Amazon Indians use poison from arrow-poison frogs on the tips of their arrows. Find nine.

Blue and yellow macaw

Coral snakes are poisonous, so animals do not eat them. Spot three.

Spider monkeys are expert tree-climbers. Their tails help them hold on. Find three.

Many kinds of parrots live in the forest. Find one of each kind.

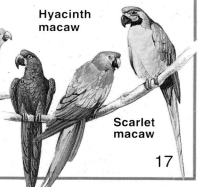

Hyacinth macaw

Golden conure

Scarlet macaw

Hot and dry

Deserts are the hottest, driest places on Earth. This picture shows part of the Sahara, the biggest desert in the world. You might be surprised by how many animals manage to live here. Can you find 124?

Fennec foxes even hear insects moving with their huge ears. Find four foxes.

Toad-headed agamid lizard. Spot four.

Desert hedgehogs **try** and keep out of the sun. Find four hedgehogs.

Mauritanian toad. Spot one.

Desert hares **sit** in the shade during the heat of the day. Find four hares.

Coursers **can run** fast to escape from enemies. Find four coursers.

Sahara gecko. Spot one.

Jerboas **hop across** the sand like mini-kangaroos. Spot five.

Sand vipers **bury** themselves deep in the sand to stay cool. Find four vipers.

Desert centipede. Spot three.

Find one sandgrouse and her three chicks.

Darkling beetle. Spot three.

Skinks are hard to spot in the desert sand. Find four skinks.

Tiger beetles make a tasty snack for some desert animals. Spot three.

Little owl. Spot four.

Sand cats hunt smaller animals. Their fur blends in with the sand. Spot four cats.

Desert locusts. Find four.

Sidewinders slither along with an S-shaped wiggle. Find four sidewinders.

Scorpions sting animals with their poisonous tails. Spot three scorpions.

These animals don't mind the heat. They hardly need anything to drink.

Addax. Find five.

Dorcas gazelle. Spot eight.

Oryx. Spot ten.

Barbary sheep. Spot 20.

Lanner falcon. Find two.

Sand rat. Spot three.

19

Female elephants and babies live together. Male elephants live alone. Find seven.

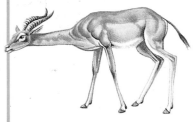

Cheetahs run faster than any other animal, but they can't do it for long. Spot two.

Gerenuks can stand up on their back legs to reach the tastiest food. Spot two.

When vultures are flying, they can spot a meal a long way away. Spot nine vultures.

African plains

Ostriches are birds, but they can't fly. Find three ostriches and their nest.

Many of the world's best-known animals live in Africa, on huge, grassy plains. There are 17 kinds of animals here.

If you look closely, you can see what each kind eats. Most eat grass and leaves. Some kill other animals to eat.

Big groups of wildebeest wander across the plains, looking for food. Find eight.

If enemies attack rhinos, they charge at them, horn first. Spot three rhinos.

Baboon babies often ride on their parents' backs. Find eight baboons.

Hippos enjoy soaking in mud. It stops their skin from drying out. Find six.

Giraffes can reach food that no other animal can get to. Find four giraffes.

If a zebra sees an enemy, it barks, to warn the others. Spot eight zebras.

Warthogs snuffle along, digging up food with their long tusks. Spot three warthogs.

Wild dogs roam the plains, searching for something to eat. Spot eight.

Thomson's gazelles jump and flash their white bottoms to confuse enemies. Spot ten.

Leopards often drag their food up into a tree to eat it in peace. Find two leopards.

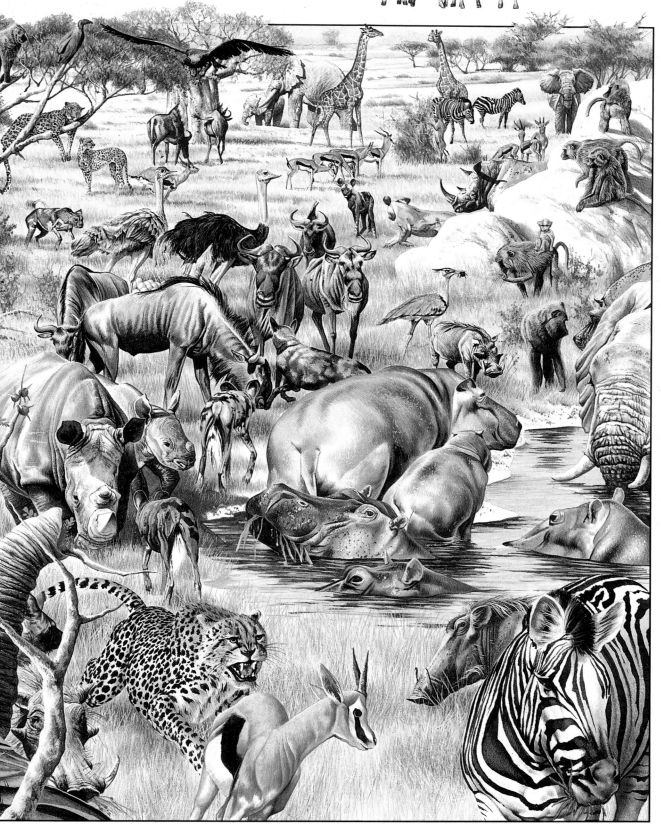

Male lions look fierce, but lionesses do the most hunting. Spot six lions.

Lioness

Lion

Kori bustards are the heaviest flying birds on Earth. Can you find two bustards here?

Hidden homes

Spotted fallow deer are hard to see in the shadowy woods. Spot six deer.

Weasels often move into a home that another animal has left. Spot four weasels.

Magpies make messy nests and a lot of noise. Can you spot two magpies here?

Dormice sleep all winter. When they wake up, they start building a home. Spot five.

Moles tunnel underground. They are almost blind. Spot one.

Woods like this are busy places in the spring. Many animals and birds are making homes for their babies.

There are 18 different kinds of animals in this wood. Can you spot where each kind makes their home?

Wild boar babies are hard to see in the long grass in the woods. Can you spot eight boars?

When a shrew family goes out, each shrew holds on to the one in front. Spot ten.

Jays bury acorns in winter. In spring, they dig them up to eat. Spot four.

Woodpeckers grip trees with their claws while they eat insects. Find four.

Several rabbit families live together in one home. Spot nine rabbits.

Badgers only come out when it is getting dark. Can you spot four badgers?

Nightjars sit still all day. Their feathers blend well with the woods. Spot two.

Squirrels build one home for winter and another for summer. Spot four squirrels.

Tawny owls fly silently. They can catch animals without being heard. Spot three.

Both fox parents look after, and teach, their cubs. Can you spot five foxes?

Horseshoe bats only start coming out of their homes as darkness falls. Spot ten.

Male

Female

Stag beetles. Spot two.

If hedgehogs are scared, they roll up into a tough, spiny ball. Spot four hedgehogs.

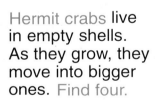

Most starfish have five arms. If one breaks off, they grow a new one. Spot five.

By the sea

Rotting seaweed is a tasty meal for sandhoppers Can you spot some sandhoppers?

Redshank use their long, thin beaks to find worms in the mud. Spot three.

Hermit crabs live in empty shells. As they grow, they move into bigger ones. Find four.

Spiny sea urchins push themselves along with their tough spikes. Spot three.

Many people visit beaches, but do they know that thousands of animals live under the sand, in pools of seawater or on the cliffs?

The sea covers this beach, and goes out again, twice every day. When it is out, the beach looks like this. Can you spot 145 animals?

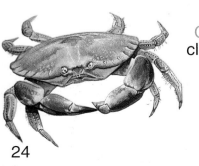

Crabs use their big claws to catch food. They can walk sideways, too. Spot six.

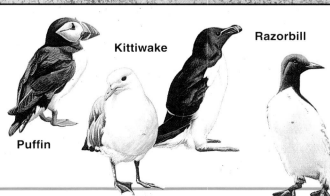

Puffin

Kittiwake

Razorbill

Guillemot

Many birds build their nests on the cliffs. Can you spot ten of each of these kinds?

Acorn barnacles grow hard coats around themselves. Can you find some here?

Lobsters are shy, but can give a nasty pinch with their big front claws. Spot two.

Cormorants stand with their wings open to dry their feathers. Find three.

A snakelocks anemone simply splits in half to make two anemones. Find ten here.

Prawns use their long feelers to search for tiny creatures to eat. Find ten prawns.

On land, beadlet anemones look like blobs. In water, they look like this. Spot five.

Many seashore animals live in hard shells. Spot ten of each of these four kinds.

Mussel **Limpet**

Common Periwinkle **Dog whelk**

Blennies hide in wet places while the sea is out. Spot six.

Oystercatchers knock shellfish off rocks with their sharp beaks. Can you spot six?

Mountains

Snow leopards, or ounces, hunt at night. They are harder to spot then. Find four.

Himalayan ibexes can clamber up slippery slopes to find food. Spot ten ibexes.

You can probably smell a takin before you see it. They smell oily. Spot two.

Male markhors spend the summer away from the females. Spot three males.

Life is not easy high up in the mountains. It's cold and windy, and the ground is often covered with snow.

The 83 animals here live in the Himalayas, the highest mountains in the world. Can you spot them all?

Himalayan black bears live in forests on the mountain slopes. Find three.

Wallcreepers climb down slopes head first. Their claws help them grip. Spot four.

Apollo butterfly. Find three.

If an animal dies, Himalayan griffon vultures swoop down and eat it. Spot six vultures.

Pikas let plants dry in the sun, then store them to eat in winter. Find six pikas.

Lammergeiers fly above the mountains, looking for dead animals to eat. Spot three.

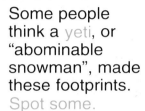

Yaks have a coat of short fur, with long, shaggy hair on top to keep warm. Find five.

Some people think a yeti, or "abominable snowman", made these footprints. Spot some.

Male tahrs have thick fur and a collar of long hair around their heads. Spot three.

While a group of bharals is eating, one keeps a look out for enemies. Spot two.

Alpine choughs push dead insects into cracks in rocks, to eat later. Spot ten choughs.

Marmots sleep in a burrow all winter. They block the door with grass to stay warm. Spot six.

Golden eagles are strong enough to carry off a baby deer. Spot two eagles.

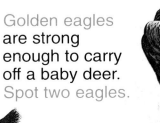

Light and dark

Indian tailor-birds sew nests from leaves and grass. Spot three.

Tigers creep up behind animals. They leap on their backs and kill them. Find one.

Great Indian hornbills like this one use their big beaks to reach any hidden fruit.

Giant flying squirrels glide silently between the jungle trees. Can you spot one?

Gavials catch fish by sweeping their long jaws from side to side. Spot three.

Indian elephants often march through the jungle in a line. Find four elephants.

Thick, hot rainforests are often called jungles. The story 'Jungle Book' is set in a jungle like this one, in India. These pictures show the jungle by day and at night. Look at both of them and try to spot which of these animals come out during the day and which at night.

Peacock

Peahen

Male peacocks shake their tails to impress the female peahens. Find one of each.

If muntjac deer are scared, they make loud barking noises, like a dog. Find two.

Slender lorises even walk on thin twigs, like this. Find one.

Leopards are expert tree-climbers and hunters. Find one leopard.

Dholes are wild dogs. They whistle to each other to stay in touch. Can you find four?

Pangolins curl up into a tight ball. Their scaly skin protects them. Find one.

Lazy sloth bears eat insects, fruit and even flowers. Can you spot a sloth bear?

Leopard cats look like mini-leopards. They are very shy. Can you spot one?

Madras tree shrews live hidden up in the trees, eating insects. Spot one.

Mongooses are brave. They even tease, and then kill, cobras. Spot one mongoose.

Gaurs are a kind of cow. If they are scared, they whistle. Spot two.

The poison from a king cobra's bite can kill a person in half an hour. Spot one.

Bonnet macaques get their name from the tufts of hair on their heads. Spot ten.

29

Magical world

Bottlenose dolphins often leap over waves, following boats. Spot six dolphins.

If giant clams sense any danger, their huge shells shut tight. Find two giant clams.

Sea squirts. Find six.

Parrot fish use their hard lips to bite off lumps of coral to eat. Spot two parrot fish.

Sea cucumber. Spot two.

Stone fish lie on the seabed, looking like stones. Can you spot two?

Barracudas are fierce hunters, snapping up other fish. Spot three barracudas.

Clown fish can hide in poisonous anemones. Find three clown fish somewhere.

When tiny sea creatures called corals die, their skeletons are left in the sea. Over thousands of years, millions of these build up to make a reef. The biggest reef in the world is the Great Barrier Reef, near Australia. Can you spot 125 animals and fish here?

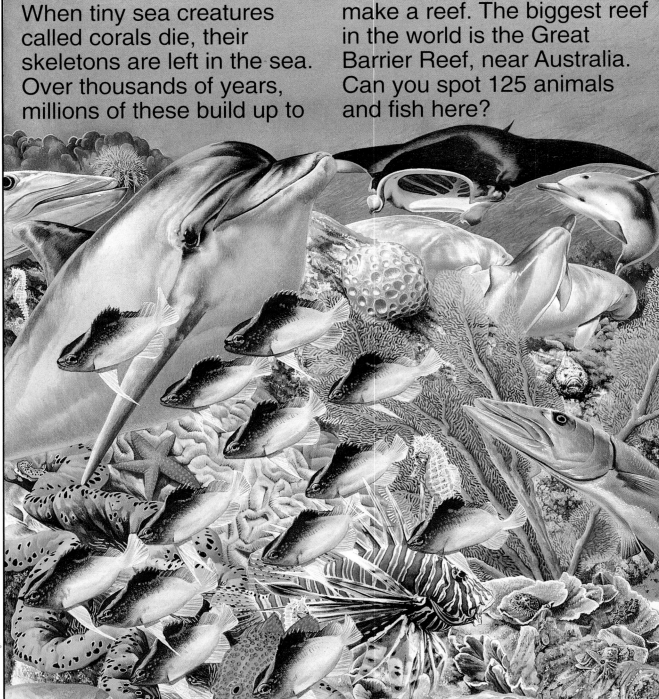

Wrasses go into other fishes' mouths and clean their teeth. Spot two.

Snapper

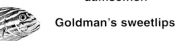

Red emperor

Blue and gold angelfish

Blue damselfish

Goldman's sweetlips

Spot which fish doesn't belong in each of these five groups.

Sea sponge. Find three.

Dugongs use their big top lip to pull plants from the seabed. Find three.

Sea horse babies grow in a pouch on their father's tummy. Spot six sea horses.

Lion fish. Find two.

Wobbegong sharks often lie still on the seabed, looking like shaggy rugs. Find one.

Bright flame shrimps nibble bugs off fishes' skins. Spot three shrimps.

Tiger cowrie. Spot three.

Manta rays flap through the water with their mouths open, catching food. Find two.

Blue sea star. Find two.

Can you guess how strange-looking hammerhead sharks got their name? Spot one.

There are many different kinds of coral. Can you find a clump of these four kinds?

Brain coral   **Sea fan**

Staghorn coral   **Plate coral**

Crown of thorns starfish eat coral. They can destroy whole reefs. Find four starfish.

Bright sea slugs slither across the coral. Spot three of each of these kinds of slug.

Naked sea slug

Saco-glossan sea slug

Spanish dancer

Out and about

Kangaroos use their big back legs to jump high up into the air. Spot ten.

Few animals risk attacking a thorny devil. Its spiky skin is too tough. Spot four.

Marsupial moles are always digging. They rarely come above ground. Find three.

Quolls have long noses for sniffing out food, and sharp teeth to eat it with. Spot two.

Shingle-backed skinks stick their blue tongues out at enemies. Spot two.

A lot of Australia is dry land, without many trees. People call it the outback. Not much rain falls, and it's very hot.

Finding enough to eat and drink is tricky. There are 75 animals somewhere in this picture. Can you spot them?

Dingos are wild dogs. They live and hunt in a big group. Can you find six dingos?

Kookaburras sound as if they are laughing when they call to each other. Spot four.

Water-holding frogs soak up water like sponges. Spot three.

Mallee fowl lay their eggs in piles of leaves, covered with sand. Find two birds.

Frilled lizards have a fold of skin like a collar around their necks. Spot three.

Bandicoots often dig. Their babies snuggle in a safe pouch under their tummies. Spot two.

Goannas prefer to run away from their enemies than fight them. Spot three.

If echidnas are scared, they bury themselves. Only their spines show then. Spot three.

Hairy-nosed wombats live in underground burrows. Find three wombats.

Budgerigars or parakeets often fly around in a big flock. Find 20 budgerigars here.

Hopping mice usually run, but they can also hop fast on their back legs. Spot two.

Emus are fast runners, but they cannot fly at all. Can you spot three emus?

Antarctica

Sperm whales can stay underwater for an hour before coming up for air. Find one.

Emperor penguin chicks snuggle between their parents' feet. Spot a chick and five adults.

Weddell seals can stay under the freezing water for an hour. Find five.

Rockhopper penguins are good at hopping on snow and rocks. Find 80.

Crabeater seals don't eat crabs. They eat tiny sea animals called krill. Find four.

Antarctica is the coldest place on Earth. The sea is frozen nearly all year. Icy winds blow across the land.

It's hard to survive here, yet millions of birds and seals do. There are 195 animals and birds for you to find here.

Blue whales are easily the biggest animals on Earth. Can you spot one here?

Wandering albatrosses glide over the sea on their huge wings. Find one.

Macaroni penguins have feathers called crests on their heads. Spot nine.

Blue-eyed shag. Spot three.

Gentoo penguins lay their eggs in nests made of stones. Spot 21 gentoo penguins.

Ross seals live on the solid ice away from other Antarctic animals. Find four.

Baby minke whales stay with their mothers for about a year. Spot a whale and her baby.

Chinstrap penguins sometimes lay their eggs on snow. Find 12 chinstraps.

Leopard seals catch penguins jumping into the sea. Spot five leopard seals.

Skuas fly over penguins' nests, waiting to kill their chicks. Find four skuas.

Adélie penguins leap from the sea onto the ice. Can you find 13?

Giant petrels eat so much they have to make themselves sick before taking off. Find four petrels.

King penguins lay one egg. Both parents guard it. Spot ten.

Male elephant seals fight to see who is stronger. Find ten elephant seals.

A closer look

Small white butterfly

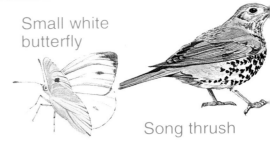

Song thrush

Tips

🌸 Birds often come to a garden with a bird-table. They like eating cheese, seeds, fat and nuts.

🌸 Lots of animals live in a pond. Others bathe in it, drink from it, or come to catch the animals in it.

🌸 A "wild" patch of garden is a great place for insects to hide. Wild flowers might grow there, too.

🌸 Berries on plants give birds a tasty meal. Plants that climb walls give them a nesting spot.

🌸 Butterflies love bright flowers which smell beautiful. Try planting some in your garden.

🌸 Flowerpots make a good home for some animals. Logs are handy for them to shelter under, too.

Animals don't only live in wild places. Lots live in gardens, like this one. There are 31 different kinds here. Can you find two of each? On this page, there are ideas for things which may make more animals visit your garden.

Garden spider

Robin

Small tortoiseshell butterfly

Vole

Bumblebee

Blackbird

Snail

Earthworm

Wren

Dragonfly

Wood mouse

Woodlouse

Newt

Magpie

Red admiral
butterfly

Hedgehog

Centipede

Greenfinch

Earwig

Frog

Slug

Chaffinch

Bullfinch

Peacock
butterfly

Toad

Wasp

Mole

Millipede

37

On the farm

Baby turkeys are called poults. Find three turkey poults.

Farmers keep cows for their milk. A cow's baby is called a calf. Can you spot a calf?

Farmers train sheepdogs to help them control their sheep. Find three sheepdog puppies.

Shetland ponies are small but they are hard workers. Find a Shetland foal.

Rats often steal other animals' food. Some farmers poison them. Spot three baby rats.

Farmers keep goats for their milk. Baby goats are called kids Spot two kids.

Farmers keep animals for their milk, meat, wool or eggs. Wild animals live on farms too. There are 19 kinds of animals in this picture. Each one has some babies hidden somewhere. Can you match the babies to the animals?

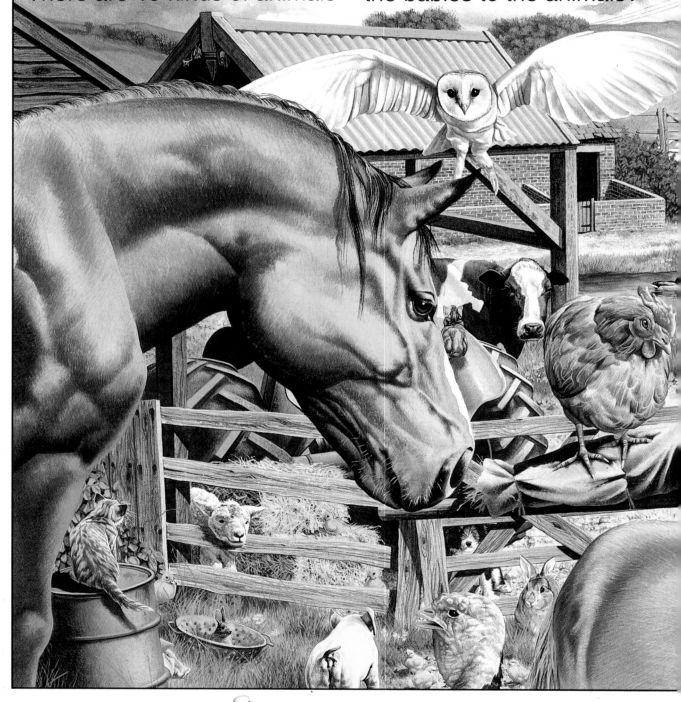

Crows eat crops, so farmers make scarecrows to scare them off. Find a baby crow.

Baby geese are called goslings. Feathers called down keep them warm. Find three.

Mice often build their nests in unusual places. Can you find four baby mice?

Cats catch mice and rats. Find three baby cats, or kittens.

Ducks swim on ponds. Find four baby ducks, or ducklings.

Bats sleep all day. Their babies eat at night. Spot two babies.

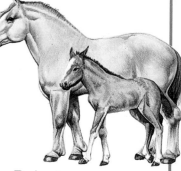

Baby horses are called foals. Shire horses work hard on farms. Find a shire foal.

Some chickens live inside, others roam outside. Can you spot three chicks?

Pigs roll in muck, but like clean straw to sleep on. Find four baby pigs, or piglets.

Many farmers keep donkeys to carry loads. Spot one baby donkey, or foal.

Rabbits live in underground burrows. Spot three baby rabbits.

Barn owls hunt at night, swooping on mice and rats. Spot two owl chicks.

Baby sheep are called lambs They are born in the spring. Find two lambs.

39

Back in time 4-5

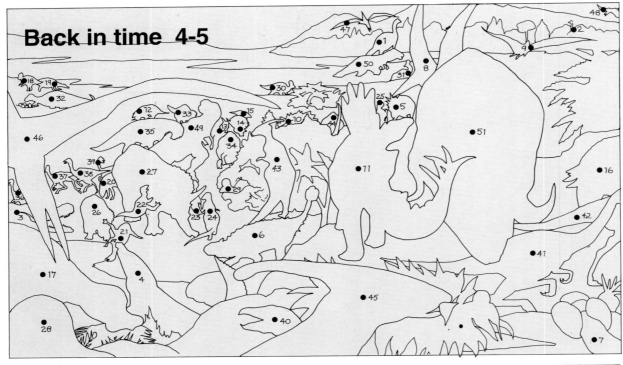

Alamosaurus 1 2
Deinosuchus 3 4
Styracosaurus 5
Ankylosaurus 6 7
Quetzalcoatlus 8 9
Stegosaurus 10 11
Panoplosaurus
12 13 14 15 16
Anatosaurus
17 18 19
Dromaeosaurus
20 21 22 23 24 25
Triceratops 26 27
Corythosaurus
28 29 30 31
Maiasaura 32
Pachycephalosaurus
33 34 35
Struthiomimus
36 37 38 39 40
41 42
Parasaurolophus
43 44 45
Pteranodon
46 47 48
Tyrannosaurus
49 50 51

Conifer forests 6-7

Skunks 1 2 3
Long-eared owls
4 5 6 7
Beavers 8 9 10
11 12 13 14 15
Crossbills 16 17
Moose
18 19 20 21 22 23
Fishers
24 25 26 27
Brown bears
28 29 30
Flying squirrels
31 32 33 34 35
Mink 36 37 38
Porcupines
39 40 41
Ospreys 42 43 44
Pumas 45 46 47
Northern shrikes
48 49
Chipmunks 50 51
52 53 54 55 56 57
Martens 58 59 60
Wolverines
61 62 63
Spruce grouse
64 65 66 67
Lynxes 68 69 70
Snowshoe hares
71 72 73 74 75 76
Black bears
77 78 79 80

Steamy swamps 8-9

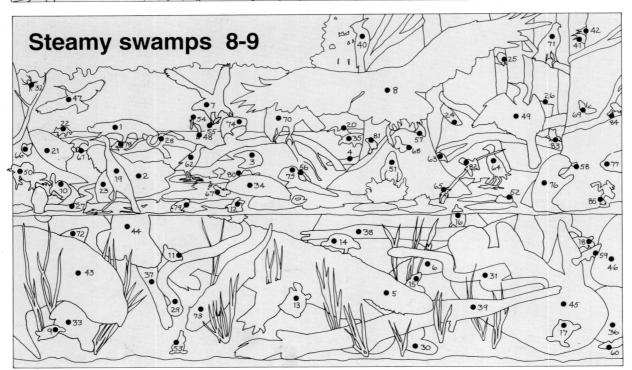

Alligators
1 2 3 4 5 6
Bald eagles 7 8
Terrapins
9 10 11 12 13
14 15 16 17 18
Little blue herons
19 20
Raccoons
21 22 23 24 25 26
Cottonmouth
snakes
27 28 29 30 31
Orb web spider 32
Snapping turtles
33 34 35 36
Garpikes 37 38 39
Pileated
woodpeckers
40 41 42
Manatees
43 44 45 46
Anhingas
47 48 49
Bullfrogs 50 51 52
Gambusia fish
53 54 55 56 57
58 59 60
Gallinules
61 62 63 64
Fisher spider 65
Zebra butterfly
66 67 68 69
Snail kites 70 71

Otters 72 73 74
75 76 77
Green tree frogs
78 79 80 81 82
83 84 85

Dusty deserts 10-11

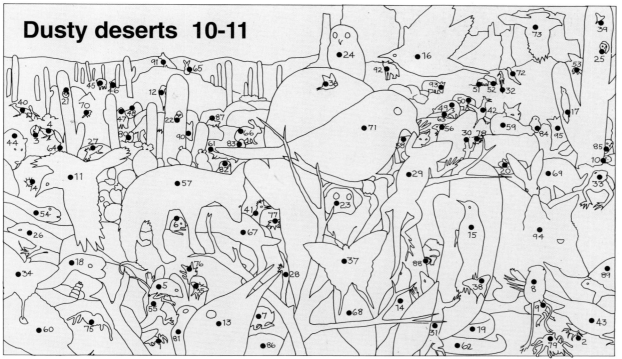

Trapdoor spiders
1 2
Gambel's quails
3 4
Kangaroo rats
5 6 7 8 9 10
Gila woodpeckers
11 12 13 14 15 16
17
Rattlesnakes
18 19 20
Elf owls
21 22 23 24 25
Fringe-toed
lizards 26 27 28
29 30 31 32 33
Swallowtail
butterflies
34 35 36 37 38 39
Roadrunners
40 41 42 43
Peccaries 44 45
46 47 48 49 50 51
52 53
Chuckwallas
54 55 56
Kit foxes 57 58 59
Gila monsters
60 61 62 63
Jackrabbits
64 65 66 67 68 69
Loggerhead
shrikes
70 71 72 73

Tarantulas 74 75
76 77 78 79
Burrowing owls
80 81 82 83 84
85
Desert tortoises
86 87 88 89
Coyotes 90 91
92 93 94 95

The Arctic 12-13

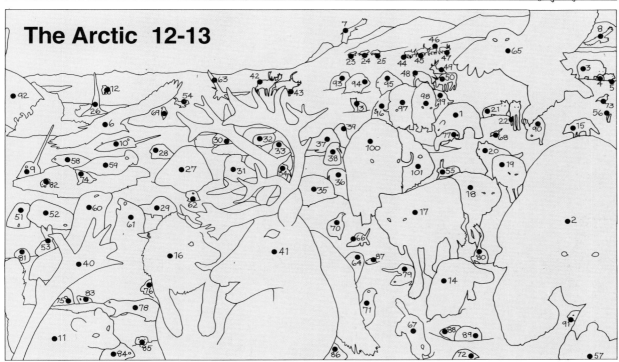

Polar bears
1 2 3 4 5
Ravens 6 7 8
Narwhals 9 10
Arctic foxes
11 12 13 14 15
Wolves
16 17 18 19 20
21 22 23 24 25
Killer whales
26 27
Walruses
28 29 30 31 32 33
34 35 36 37 38 39
Caribou
40 41 42 43 44 45
46 47 48 49 50
Beluga whales
51 52
Arctic hares
53 54 55 56 57
Ribbon seal 58
Hooded seal 59
Harp seal 60
Ringed seal 61
Bearded seal 62
Snowy owls
63 64 65
Arctic ground
squirrels 66 67 68
Ptarmigans
69 70 71 72 73
Baby seals
74 75 76 77

Stoats 78 79 80
Lemmings 81 82
83 84 85 86 87
88 89 90 91
Humpback whale
92
Musk oxen
93 94 95 96 97
98 99 100 101

Under the sea 14-15

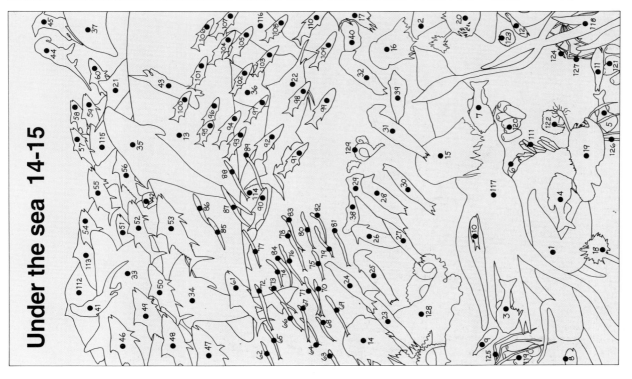

Gulper eels 1 2
Hatchet fish
3 4 5 6 7
Lantern fish
8 9 10 11 12
Fin whale 13
Jellyfish
14 15 16 17
Angler fish
18 19 20
Marlin 21 22
Squid
23 24 25 26 27
28 29 30 31 32
Basking shark 33
Dolphins
34 35 36 37
Skates 38 39 40
Sea otters
41 42 43 44 45
Tuna 46 47 48
49 50 51 52 53
54 55 56 57 58
59 60 61
Sand eels
62 63 64 65 66
67 68 69 70 71
72 73 74 75 76
77 78 79 80 81
82 83 84 85 86
87 88 89
Herring
90 91 92 93 94
95 96 97 98 99

100 101 102 103
104 105 106 107
108 109 110
Beardworms 111
Dall's porpoises
112 113 114 115
116
Giant squid
117 118
Sponges
119 120 121
Sea lilies
122 123 124
Sea spiders
125 126 127
Octopuses
128 129

Rainforests 16-17

Hoatzins 1 2 3
Capybaras 4 5 6
7 8 9 10 11 12 13
Golden lion
tamarins
14 15 16
Cocks-of-the-rock
17 18
Jaguar 19
Anacondas
20 21 22
Giant armadillos
23 24
Arrow-poison
frogs 25 26 27 28
29 30 31 32 33
Blue and yellow
macaw 34
Scarlet macaw 35
Hyacinth macaw
36
Golden conure 37
Spider monkeys
38 39 40
Coral snakes
41 42 43
Silky anteaters
44 45
Howler monkeys
46 47 48 49
Toucans
50 51 52 53
Hummingbirds
54 55 56

Sloths 57 58 59
Uakari monkeys
60 61 62
63 64 65
Emerald tree
boas 66 67 68
Tapirs 69 70 71

Hot and dry 18-19

Camels
1 2 3 4 5 6 7 8 9
Desert
centipedes
10 11 12
Sandgrouse
13 14 15 16
Darkling beetles
17 18 19
Skinks
20 21 22 23
Tiger beetles
24 25 26
Toad-headed
lizards
27 28 29 30
Sand cats
31 32 33 34
Desert locusts
35 36 37 38
Sidewinders
39 40 41 42
Scorpions
43 44 45
Sand rats
46 47 48
Lanner falcons
49 50
Oryxes
51 52 53 54 55
56 57 58 59 60
Addaxes
61 62 63 64 65

Barbary sheep
66 67 68 69 70
71 72 73 74 75
76 77 78 79 80
81 82 83 84 85
Dorcas gazelles
86 87 88 89 90
91 92 93
Sand vipers
94 95 96 97
Jerboas 98 99
100 101 102
Sahara gecko
103
Coursers
104 105 106 107
Desert hares
108 109 110 111
Mauritanian toad
112
Desert
hedgehogs
113 114 115 116
Little owls
117 118 119 120
Fennec foxes
121 122 123 124

African plains 20-21

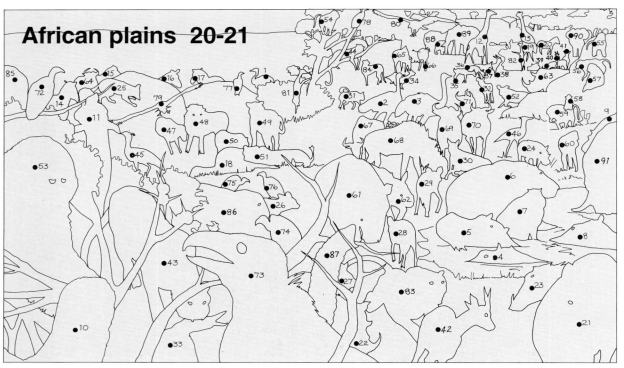

Ostriches 1 2 3
Hippos
4 5 6 7 8 9
Giraffes
10 11 12 13
Zebras 14 15 16
17 18 19 20 21
Warthogs
22 23 24
Wild dogs 25 26
27 28 29 30 31 32
Thomson's
gazelles
33 34 35 36 37
38 39 40 41 42
Leopards 43 44
Kori bustards
45 46
Lions
47 48 49 50 51 52
Baboons 53 54
Rhinos 61 62 63
Wildebeest 64 65
66 67 68 69 70 71
Vultures 72 73 74
75 76 77 78 79 80
Gerenuks 81 82
Cheetahs 83 84
Elephants 85 86
87 88 89 90 91

Hidden homes 22-23

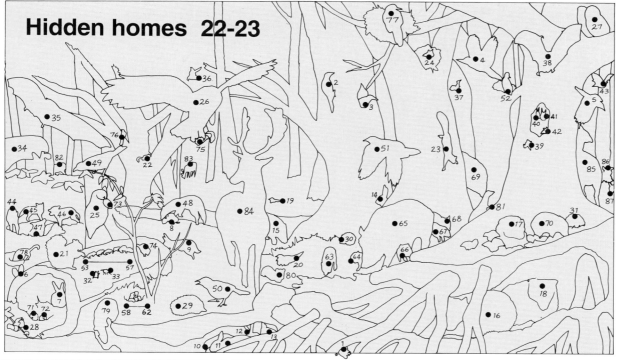

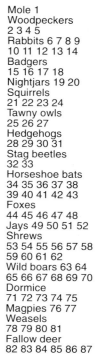

Mole 1
Woodpeckers
2 3 4 5
Rabbits 6 7 8 9
10 11 12 13 14
Badgers
15 16 17 18
Nightjars 19 20
Squirrels
21 22 23 24
Tawny owls
25 26 27
Hedgehogs
28 29 30 31
Stag beetles
32 33
Horseshoe bats
34 35 36 37 38
39 40 41 42 43
Foxes
44 45 46 47 48
Jays 49 50 51 52
Shrews
53 54 55 56 57 58
59 60 61 62
Wild boars 63 64
65 66 67 68 69 70
Dormice
71 72 73 74 75
Magpies 76 77
Weasels
78 79 80 81
Fallow deer
82 83 84 85 86 87

By the sea 24-25

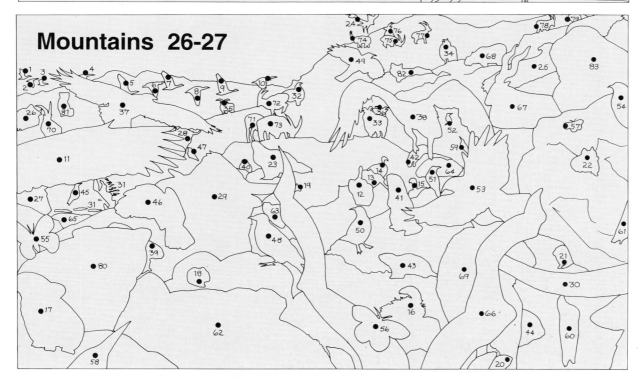

Sandhoppers 1
Barnacles 2
Lobsters 3 4
Cormorants
5 6 7
Snakelocks
anemones
8 9 10 11 12 13
14 15 16 17
Prawns
18 19 20 21 22
23 24 25 26 27
Beadlet
anemones
28 29 30 31 32
Oystercatchers
33 34 35 36 37 38
Blennies
39 40 41 42 43 44
Mussels
45 46 47 48 49
50 51 52 53 54
Limpets
55 56 57 58 59
60 61 62 63 64
Periwinkles
65 66 67 68 69
70 71 72 73 74
Dog whelks
75 76 77 78 79
80 81 82 83 84
Puffins
85 86 87 88 89
90 91 92 93 94

Guillemots 95
96 97 98 99 100
101 102 103 104
Kittiwakes
105 106 107 108
109 110 111 112
113 114
Razorbills
115 116 117 118
119 120 121 122
123 124
Crabs 125 126
127 128 129 130
Sea urchins
131 132 133
Hermit crabs
134 135 136 137
Redshanks
138 139 140
Starfish
141 142 143
144 145

Mountains 26-27

Bar-headed
geese 1 2 3 4 5 6
7 8 9 10
Griffon vultures
11 12 13 14 15 16
Pikas
17 18 19 20 21 22
Lammergeiers
23 24 25
Yaks
26 27 28 29 30
Yeti/abominable
snowman
footprints 31
Tahrs 32 33 34
Bharals 35 36
Golden eagles
37 38
Marmots
39 40 41 42 43 44
Alpine choughs
45 46 47 48 49
50 51 52 53 54
Apollo butterflies
55 56 57
Wallcreepers
58 59 60 61
Black bears
62 63 64
Markhors
65 66 67
Takins
68 69
Ibexes 70 71 72

73 74 75 76 77
78 79
Snow leopards
80 81 82 83

Light and dark 28-29

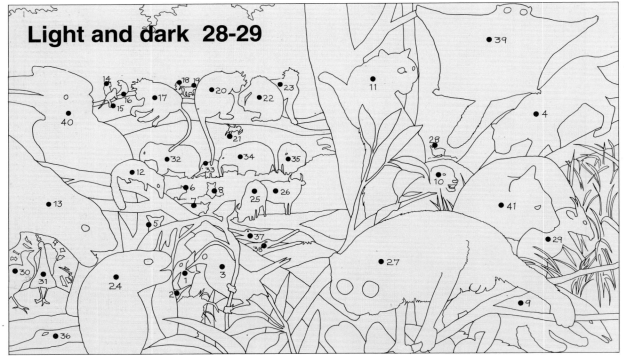

Tailor-birds
1 2 3
Leopard 4
Dholes 5 6 7 8
Pangolin 9
Sloth bear 10
Leopard cat 11
Madras tree shrew
12
Mongoose 13
Macaques
14 15 16 17 18 19
20 21 22 23
King cobra 24
Gaurs 25 26
Slender loris 27
Muntjac deer
28 29
Peacock/peahen
30 31
Elephants
32 33 34 35
Gavials
36 37 38
Giant flying
squirrel 39
Hornbill 40
Tiger 41

Magical world 30-31

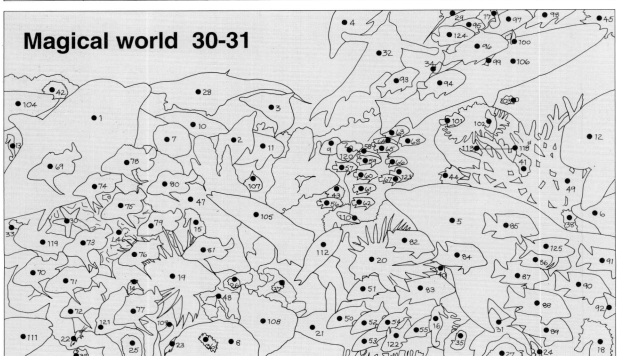

Bottlenose
dolphins
1 2 3 4 5 6
Sea sponges
7 8 9
Dugongs
10 11 12
Sea horses 13
14 15 16 17 18
Lion fish 19 20
Wobbegong 21
Flame shrimps
22 23 24
Tiger cowries
25 26 27
Manta rays
28 29
Blue sea stars
30 31
Hammerhead
shark 32
Naked sea slugs
33 34 35
Sacoglossan
sea slugs
36 37 38
Spanish dancers
39 40 41
Crown of thorns
42 43 44 45
Brain coral 46
Sea fan 47
Plate coral 48
Staghorn coral 49

Snappers 50 51
52 53 54 55
Angelfish
56 57 58 59 60
61 62 63 64 65
66 67 68
Damselfish
69 70 71 72 73
74 75 76 77 78
79 80 81
Red emperors
82 83 84 85 86
87 88 89 90 91
92
Sweetlips 93 94
95 96 97 98
Wrasses 99 100
Clown fish
101 102 103
Barracudas
104 105 106
Stone fish
107 108
Sea cucumber
109 110
Parrot fish
111 112
Sea squirts
113 114 115 116
117 118
Giant clams
119 120
'Odd' fish 121
122 123 124 125

Out and about 32-33

Shingle-backed
skinks 1 2
Mallee fowl 3 4
Frilled lizards
5 6 7
Bandicoots 8 9
Goannas 10 11 12
Echidnas 13 14 15
Wombats 16 17 18
Emus 19 20 21
Hopping mice
22 23
Budgerigars/
parakeets 24 25
26 27 28 29 30 31
32 33 34 35 36 37
38 39 40 41 42 43
Water-holding
frogs 44 45 46
Kookaburras
47 48 49 50
Dingos
51 52 53 54 55 56
Quolls 57 58
Marsupial moles
59 60 61
Thorny devils
62 63 64 65
Kangaroos
66 67 68 69 70
71 72 73 74 75

Antarctica 34-35

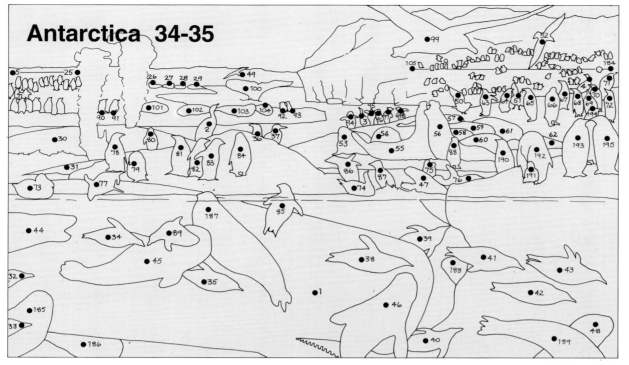

Sperm whale 1
Shags 2 3 4
Gentoo penguins
5 6 7 8 9 10 11
12 13 14 15 16
17 18 19 20 21
22 23 24 25
Ross seals
26 27 28 29
Minke whales
30 31
Chinstrap
penguins 32 33
34 35 36 37 38
39 40 41 42 43
Leopard seals
44 45 46 47 48
Skuas
49 50 51 52
Elephant seals
53 54 55 56 57
58 59 60 61 62
King penguins
63 64 65 66 67
68 69 70 71 72
Giant petrels
73 74 75 76
Adélie penguins
77 78 79 80 81
82 83 84 85 86
87 88 89
Macaroni
penguins 90 91 92
93 94 95 96 97 98

Albatross 99
Blue whale 100
Crabeater seals
101 102 103 104
Rockhopper
penguins
105 106 107 108
109 110 111 112
113 114 115 116
117 118 119 120
121 122 123 124
125 126 127 128
129 130 131 132
133 134 135 136
137 138 139 140
141 142 143 144
145 146 147 148
149 150 151 152
153 154 155 156
157 158 159 160
161 162 163 164
165 166 167 168
169 170 171 172
173 174 175 176
177 178 179 180
181 182 183 184
Weddell seals
185 186 187 188
189
Emperor
penguins 190 191
192 193 194 195

A closer look 36-37

Foxes 1 2
Small white
butterflies 3 4
Song thrushes
5 6
Earthworms 7 8
Wrens 9 10
Dragonflies
11 12
Wood mice
13 14
Woodlice 15 16
Newts 17 18
Magpies 19 20
Red admiral
butterflies 21 22
Hedgehogs
23 24
Centipedes
25 26
Greenfinches
27 28
Earwigs 29 30
Frogs 31 32
Slugs 33 34
Chaffinches
35 36
Millipedes 37 38
Moles 39 40
Wasps 41 42
Toads 43 44
Peacock
butterflies 45 46
Bullfinches 47 48

Snails 49 50
Blackbirds 51 52
Bumblebees
53 54
Voles 55 56
Small tortoise-
shell butterflies
57 58
Robins 59 60
Garden spiders
61 62

On the farm 38-39

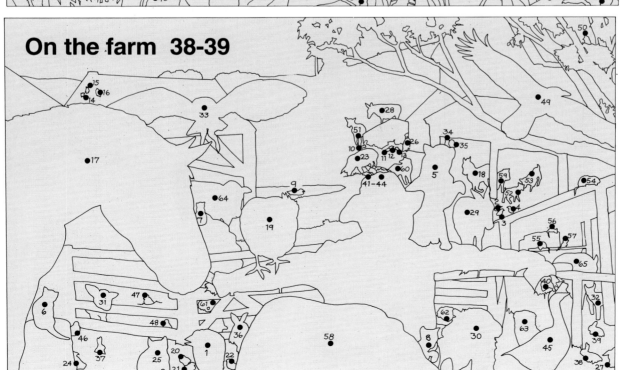

Turkey 1
Turkey poults
2 3 4
Cat 5
Kittens 6 7 8
Duck 9
Ducklings
10 11 12 13
Baby bats 14 15
Bat 16
Shire horse 17
Shire foal 18
Chicken 19
Chicks 20 21 22
Pig 23
Piglets
24 25 26 27
Donkey 28
Donkey foal 29
Sheep 30
Lambs 31 32
Barn owl 33
Owl chicks 34 35
Rabbit 36
Baby rabbits
37 38 39
Mouse 40
Baby mice
41 42 43 44
Goose 45
Goslings
46 47 48
Crow 49
Baby crow 50

Goat 51
Goat kids 52 53
Rat 54
Baby rats
55 56 57
Shetland pony 58
Shetland foal 59
Sheepdog 60
Puppies 61 62 63
Cow 64
Calf 65

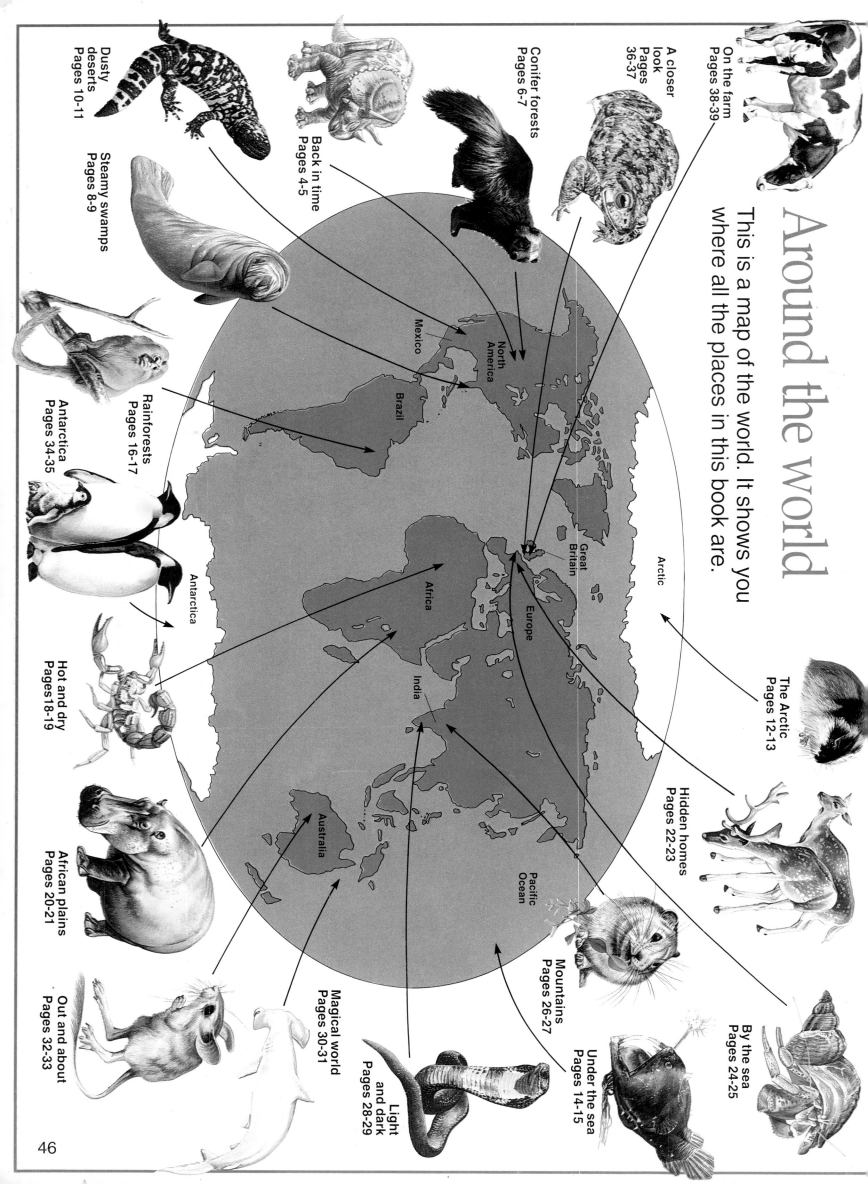

Around the world

This is a map of the world. It shows you where all the places in this book are.

Mexico

North America

Brazil

Africa

Great Britain

Europe

Arctic

India

Pacific Ocean

Australia

Antarctica

Index

The page numbers next to the animals' names in this index show where to find information about them, not just a picture.